Openings 42
The Poetry Society of the Open University

Annual Anthology

of

OU Poets

2025

Copyright remains with the individual poets.
All rights reserved.

Published 2025 by Open University Poets.

ISBN 978-1-7399361-4-3

Editor: Sue Spiers
Cover: https://www.publicdomainpictures.net/pictures/500000/velka/cormorant-japanese-vintage-art 16762886657mg.jpg Karen Arnold

Printed by Lulu.com

Introduction

OU Poets is the Poetry Society of the Open University. It is open to any student or staff member, past or present. At the time of going to press there are about 90 members from all over the U.K. with some in mainland Europe and worldwide.

Members of the society submit poems to a magazine, which is produced 5 times a year, each one having a different voluntary editor. The magazine is not a publication *per se* and is strictly produced by the members for the members. There is a section for comment and criticism of members' work.

At the end of the year, members are asked to vote for the 20 poems they most appreciated from the 5 magazines produced that year. Those with the most votes, allowing for no more than one poem per poet, appear in the following year's issue of Openings. The anthology is as broad-based as the society itself and reflects the varied backgrounds, interests and tastes of the members.

If you would like more information about OU Poets, please contact the Secretary:
Sally Evans
secretary@oupoets.org.uk

or the Chair:
Karen Macfarlane
chair@oupoets.org.uk

Or visit our website at http://www.oupoets.org.uk

 @OUPoets

Contents

Poem	Name	Page
Skiddaw, October 2024	Ross McGivern	7
The Grey	Pip Adwin	9
When You Need Courage for the Year Ahead	Karen Macfarlane	10
The Sea Widow - Part 2	Kewal Paigankar	13
A Prophecy	Jacob Lund	14
Newspaper Suit	Geoff Chilton	15
Un Bel Di	Ian Campbell	16
Home and Away	Ian Simmonds	17
The Clock at the Front of the Station in Slough	Phil Craddock	18
Elderly	Jenny Hamlett	20
Ancient Wonders	Cate Cody	22
Unattainable	Helen Hunniset	23
Just Another Day	Dee Richards	24
A Male Bond	Tim Field	26
The March	K. J. Barrett	27
Rendezvous	Kate Young	28
For Marnie	Tony Sutton	29
Maybe it's time for a cull	Suzie Millar	31
The Old Ford	Jim Lindop	32

Contents

Poem	Name	Page
The House where I was Born	Barbara Cumbers	33
Double Acrostic Sonnet	Steve Francis	34
Note to Self	Nigel Kent	35
Misericord	Ivan McGuinness	36
Lenny and Lisa	Denis Ahern	37
Boppng at the Rose and Crown	Polly Stretton	38
Roles of Fat	Liz Beber	40
Addressing Sylvia Plath's Fan Club	Sue Spiers	42
Best Friends	Alice Harrison	43
Mothers and Daughters	Sally James	45
Solo	Wendy Goulstone	46
At the Philharmonic	Adrian Green	47
Starlings	Katherine Rawlings	48
What Gifts?	M. C. Gardner	49
A Whisper of Heavy Wings	Dan Sarkozi	50
Cormorant	Julie Anne Gilligan	51
A Djinn-eyed Clan	Sally Evans	52
Ode to an Opossum	Susan Jarvis Bryant	53
Acknowledgements		56

For Kevin John Barrett
(13/09/1949 - 07/03/2025)

Ross McGivern

Skiddaw, October 2024

Slate
path, slate
skies, boots scrunch
a marcher's rhythm, hikers
poles tap the hi-hat flourish.
Inbound fog devours her hi-vis, the
mountain's silence consumes the crisp
packet rustle of her waterproofs. Scree
burrows deep into wool and leather. Slate
mountain, slate centuries, feet mill grit
further into tracks worn by hobnails and hooves.
Surgical metal threaded into bone, industrial metal
screwed deep into cairns. Laminate map, laminated
mudstone. Compass and condensation, droplets obscure
maps, sodden seams imprint thighs, rain pools like tarns in
puckered sleeves. Stumbling onwards to touch the battered trig.
Predatory drops lurk beyond mist-stolen ridges. Cragged soles,
slaked skin, water finds the careless inch left between gaiter,
tongue and lace. At nine hundred and thirty-one metres,
we summit alone in foggish-cloud. At nine hundred
and thirty-one metres, we cannot escape the rain,
we meet precipitation at source. We are the rain.
Scar path, lactic calves. Drugged up, dragged
down Skiddaw's weathered vein, a stone
serpent striking over Derwent. We
descend from ambition, trip over
multiplying stones, slander rusted,
arthritic ankles. We've bagged
our mountain. Four years of
waiting for the perfect day

that does not exist in late
October. Slate shoes or
even hobnail and
hooves, please
carry me
home.

Pip Adwin

The Grey

On Sundays the ferry took us back to school
and once, in a gale so strong we were probably a sacrifice
to some heathen, Viking god,
I sat outside in the rain that thought it was spray
and the spray that thought it was Valkyrie tears.

The bumpy green of the deck was comfort
to my fourteen-year-old bones, and the sea
launched wave after wave after wave, high above my head
and onto the frightened cars,
shuddering in their chains.

I can still taste the grey;
and shards of orange from life savers and oilskins
bobbing like puffin beaks
in the heaving, foam flecked mess
that used to be sky and sea.

The new ferries make our old girls look like rafts.
They don't disappear under the waves,
the current doesn't push them all the way down Yell Sound
to my mother's house,
and heathen sacrifice is long since forbidden by the council.

But the grey is still the grey, and I remember –
when gods stirred the pot,
and nobody watched but me.

Karen Macfarlane

When you need courage for the year ahead (A swimmer's perspective)

After Lauren Zuniga, It's Going To Be Amazing

It's going to be cold.
Bloody cold.
Squeal when it reaches your oxters cold.
Fecking freezing.
The cold will take your breath away;
you will take it back
and exhale, slow and loud
like an old seal.

Your body will be lost
in an underworld
you don't really understand,
just your head above the surface,
hoping nothing's lurking,
keeping moving,
limbs hovering
like your own ghost below you.

Afterwards, you'll fumble with your socks,
abandon all hope of knickers,
build your woolly cocoon
until you can't bend in the middle.

Still, you may shiver,
your bones may shout in protest.
If a friend – even one
you've never met before –
hands you a biscuit
or a hot cup, take it.
The worst is over quicker
when a group generates heat.

You will do this again
and again. Some mornings,
you'll want your duvet
more than your icy lake
or frozen sands.
Sometimes there will be too much cold
and it will defeat you.
But, at some point

you'll remember the sparkles
and the shimmers
and how you breathed in the light
and it made your blood shine
like the moon on New Year's Eve,
how your skin felt unworn,
just off the production line,
able to defend you from anything.

You'll run down that beach,
across that forest floor,
to reach your waves,
your river, your loch.
You'll wade in, aware,
somewhere deep,
of thousands of others
doing the same, or dreaming of it.

You won't say much
because it's going to be cold.
The cold will take your breath away;
you will take it back.

Kewal Paigankar

The Sea Widow – part 2

Lately she had taken to
Wading into the sea
At midnight.

Sitting in front of the mirror
Brushing her hair, she'd notice
The colour changing to thick auburn
Banishing the grey,
The brows no longer furrowed,
Her dull complexion now radiant.
Even the sepia-tinged picture of Jack
In his fisherman cardigan,
Curly hair swept under a round cap,
Brightened up as it grew dark.
She looked at it every night
Before turning the lights out.

One wind-lashed night
Jack let himself in, muttering,
I left behind what I had caught
I missed what I could carry.
As the sea water rolled
Down his ankles in a curved line.

Jacob Lund

A Prophecy

He fell in love not with a god
but with the vacancy of a sleeping bag
twisted foetally in the cathedral close,
as if to return in self-mockery was comfort enough
in a lost time.

The choir faltered in their cadences
as they went in, seeing him,
their rhythms awkward,
their centuries disjointed
by this disgraced polyphony.

It was said that he himself had no tongue,
though modesty prevented proof
beyond an upturned hand made
new with sunlight, evanescent as
most offerings seem.

And, had I taken it,
that silent, broken face
of mine might have formed some words
over whatever he did not say this was:
I expect the ruins of Jerusalem.

Geoff Chilton

Newspaper Suit

Your newspaper suit
showed its disadvantages when it rained.
Broadsheets stuck to your legs,
headlines on your thighs:
cabinet minister caught in scandal.

Your jacket of tabloid sports
was football fixtures,
and the two-thirty at Newmarket.
The crossword across your groin
revealed those parts
you'd preferred to have kept covered;
four across was suggestiveness,
eight down was vulgarity.

Your trousers, slightly flared,
carried lifestyle and holidays
and letters to the editor.
But the agony pages were there,
your cherished wisdom and slight.

I watched your clothes turn to smeared ink,
blurred sans serif,
a mash of paper pulp
and the flapping wet pages
of your newspaper suit.

Ian Campbell

Un bel di

Don't let the promise of tomorrow fool you,
it may evaporate before you know,
don't let the 'maybes' and the 'what ifs' rule you,
sometimes they never come, before they go.

That fine day, that tell-tale plume of smoke on the horizon,
the vessel white, that calls, and grows in time,
the gift of love, that you feel your heart relies on,
may have less substance than a string of words in mime.

It's possible that your finest time's behind you,
as likely that true happiness is gone,
but you have memory to prompt, prick and remind you,
lucky fool, thank God for all the sunshine that has shone.

The little man, who takes the winding path towards you,
far below, he climbs the hill, that fateful day,
'Little one, my dear wife, my orange blossom,
how much I've wronged you I can't begin to say.'

Be grateful, for those moments of fulfilment,
be wary of the hours of fun to come,
mishaps delight in their concealment,
no regrets then, as you head towards the sun?

No fine day then, with the promise of perfection,
just the knowledge that some fine days have occurred,
just be thankful for that heady sweet confection
that resulted when your cup of life was stirred.

Ian Simmonds

Home and Away

In Cambrian rapture to soar once more:
an uncanny compound of spirit and place,
where pasts abide mildly in rhythmic rapport:
and infinite fusion of inherent grace.

An uncanny compound of spirit and place,
an echo of sanity: there to restore.
An infinite fusion of inherent grace,
a vital asylum that pervades every pore.

An echo of sanity: there to restore,
like a fossil's foray to primal birthplace.
A vital asylum that pervades every pore.
like a sentient relic of Earth's embrace.

Like a fossil's foray to primal birthplace,
where pasts abide mildly in rhythmic rapport:
like a sentient relic of Earth's embrace,
in Cambrian rapture to soar once more.

Phil Craddock

The Clock at the Front of the Station in Slough

The clock at the front of the station in Slough
is never displaying what time it is now.
It's sometimes behind and it's sometimes ahead
and sometimes it's some time quite different instead.

This causes confusion. Correct information
is what is required at the front of a station.
When catching a train, approaching from town
one needs to know – should one speed up or slow down?

If the clock's running fast, one thinks one is late
and rushes, then has too much time on one's plate.
If the clock's running slow, that's also deceiving:
one plods to the platform to find the train's leaving.

And if one's been shopping, and heavily laden
with food for the week (a weekly occasion)
with bags in each hand, held tight in each fist
one cannot check up on one's watch on one's wrist.

One battles the barrier, stomps up the stairs
only to find one's been caught unawares
and stifles a kind of a whistling scream
that won't have been heard since the great age of steam.

But why is it running too slow or too fast?
Why is it set in the future or past?
I venture a reason. It may not be right
but the state of the railways, it possibly might.

The clock at the front of the station in Slough
is always displaying times other than now
because it shifts time zone from hour to hour
as ownership shifts to the next foreign power.

Jenny Hamlett

Elderly

  Time
comes and goes as if
he led the Furry Dance
through Helston streets
  and pranced
in and out of my front door.

Memories, fragile
as gossamer threads,
are carelessly spread
across our kitchen floor.

They will not be organised!
  Names hide
underneath the sink,
  the word *when*
has run off with the milkman
to the south of France.

Did I send out a poem
last summer
  or yesterday
or even tomorrow?

Memories move in circles
  around my head,
cavort uncontrolled
through my thoughts.

The only certainty,
the relentless ticking
of a clock
scooping up time.

Cate Cody

Ancient wonders

They came in crumpled,
like withered, wintered leaves;
stiffened and crunched

Slowly they opened,
like a sunflower's gradual unfolding,

as they offered themselves
to the music's movements;
to its warmth and joy

and they giggled free of creaks,
turned from buckram to silk

unfurling

Ancient wonders from the care home at our monthly Daytime Dance.

Helen Hunnisett

Unattainable

Dawn brings silence, a quiet world,
no sounds of the busy biosphere,
noisy yet hushed, voiceless.

The birds sing in the morning,
but no dawn chorus greets me,
my ears receive nothing.

The blaring silence, always there,
yet every minute, every second,
a hissing radio that can't be tuned,
drum rolls, jet aeroplanes,
shrieking.

Hissing, shushing, swishing on and on,
the hearing aids come to life and ding
like Tinkerbell in my ears,
magically, miraculously, marvellously,
quieting jets, drums, and radio.

Enter muffles like hearing through a wall,
half-words, disjointed sentences,
the brain working on the meaning,
translating sounds into words, guessing.
silence does not exist.

Dee Richards

Just Another Day

A dead flower, a thorny rose,
a dead moth on some holey clothes.
A chipped mug, a broken tooth,
loose tiles on my roof.
A forgotten dentist appointment,
a cut on the hand but no available ointment.
A fallen tree, a stinging nettle,
no whistle from by brand-new kettle.
A stained leather shoe, worn out soles,
hard old butter and crumbly rolls.
A blunt knife, some mouldy bread,
springs protruding from my bed.
A chest of drawers, odd socks with no pairs,
a loose-fitting carpet on the stairs.
Out of date cheese, a buzz from the fridge,
a footpath to a river but there is no bridge.
A coat rough like sandpaper, a shirt smooth like silk,
a freshly made tea but there is no milk.
A tin opener for the beans failing to work,
a washing machine and a shrunken skirt.
An untidy lounge so where's the remote,
a playground lover without a skipping rope.
An important document, a computer crash,
an overfilled bin nowhere for the trash.
A tiring job, no time for the kids,
jars of honey without any lids.
A full memory, but an empty heart,
no sharpener for your pencil when you need it for art.

A foggy day, a clouded pint of beer,
a late postcard through the door, *I wish you were here*.
No ingredients for the cakes a recipe for disaster,
the childhood cut and a wrong sized plaster.
A crowded room, a lack of space,
an old grey hair and a wrinkled old face.
A failing engine, a petrol spill,
the passing of a person not leaving a will.

Tim Field

A Male Bond

Nothing marks my mother's grave.
No stone.
Not even a rose bush
overgrown.

No place to come and stand
and stare.
As if no-one seems to be bothered
to care.

No memorial to mark;
no bench.
No trace from her last day
hence.

Something never to be discussed
with dad;
nor with my brother, come to that.
Too sad.

Anniversaries come and go,
death, birthday.
But nothing is ever said.
We seem to prefer it that way.

K. J. Barrett

The March

I looked down on the dying face,
The eyes were closed
The mouth twisted with pain,
Fingers clutched at the hem of a cloak;
A slight vapour was rising through a grey cape
Which covered the soldier's breast,
I cast it aside;
Under his torn ribs
The lungs were exposed
The heart beating sluggishly;
A number of silver and copper medals
Which he had been wearing round his neck on a black ribbon
Were driven deep into his flesh;
We covered him up,
The soldier half opened his eyes
His lips moved,
And for the sake of something to do
I filled my morphia syringe.

After the injection
He laid his head back against the birch almost in comfort,
He closed his eyes
and already
Large flakes of snow were falling into the dark, deep sockets.

Inspired by the diaries of Hans Carossa.

Kate Young

Rendezvous

Every Friday he goes to meet her
in the secluded spot he knows well,
cellophane-clad roses in one hand,
picnic bag on his shoulder and 1970s
fold up chair tucked under his arm,
the one they chose in Woolworths,
floral design, cheap in the summer sale.

He always greets her with a smile,
unfolds the chair and settles back.
She prefers to recline on grass, restful,
refuses food, *nothing but bone*, he notes.
In between mouthfuls of ham and cheese
he tells her all about his week, witters on
while she says little, good listener though.

When he is finished, he packs the bag,
folds up the 1970s chair with floral design,
the one they chose in Woolworths,
cheap in the summer sale, and tucks it
under his arm, says, *see you next week.*
With the creak of ageing knees he stoops,
lays the cellophane-clad roses at her feet.

Tony Sutton

For Marnie

In my dream I find you there
beside the carousel.
Your little face lit up with joy
to see the horsey ready there
to take us both to *Far Away*.
I tickle you as we mount up,
ready for adventure.
Your smiles and giggles melt my heart
(and still they melt my heart today)
but so cold the light that morning brings.

So now, each night I long for dreams
because you left so young.
In those dreams we travel far,
away on painted horse.
Where magic's real and children's laughter
brings wonder to my earthly life.
Our hearts dance and our hearts sing
but cold the light that morning brings.

I'll never hold you in my arms
nor touch your golden hair.
I'll never see you all grown up
nor touch your face, nor see your smile.
But I will meet you in my dreams
and ride away on that painted horse,
play and laugh, sing and dance
until the morning comes again
with the cold light that it will bring
and a different carousel begins.

When I will keep you safe again
within my breaking, burning heart:
a broken heart that mourns for you
but a heart that burns with love for you.

And my heart melts.
And my heart melts.
And my heart melts.

So cold the light that morning brings.

Suzie Millar

Maybe it's time for a cull

Photos of people I no longer know.
Friendships been and gone.
Should I be sad or accepting
that's just how life goes, you know?

With so much of life behind me
should I bin photographic remains?
Film rolls and negatives that multiplied
I mean, why am I keeping them?

Sometimes it's fun to reminisce
laugh over olden times
but who wants to view old photos
of strangers they can barely name?

Experience has taught me that clinging on
is rarely the way to go.

If I lighten my load in the present
will the future thank me someday?

Jim Lindop

The Old Ford

As we tracked down the unloved path,
dodging the low-hanging briars
and cautious for our ageing limbs,
the memory of that old Ford
swatted at me like those earworms
that fatten in your morning head…

That day, we'd stopped our slow amble
along the bird-limed promenade,
where toy dogs pulled at pink leashes,
where strains of the calliope
singed the sea-soothed air and gulls banked
and the foreshore sang its shanties.

The Model Y Ford shuddered, sighed,
black as Newgate's knocker, and slid
into its slot…and I could see,
in my mind, that little boy, and
his granddad, tongue stuck out, driving
his old Ford to our brand-new house.

Barbara Cumbers

The house where I was born

I think of knocking, explaining, asked in
perhaps to see the new, the smart, the modern
that I'm sure is there. Doubtful, I wander
down the side, peer over the wall.
The air-raid shelter's gone of course,
the coal shed; but so are vegetable beds
and compost heaps. The garden's now
a dead expanse, paved, decked and gravelled.
Where the ash tree, my ash tree, grew
is changed as if the tree had never been.
In its place, a stylish outdoor living room.

Our house was all make-do-and-mend:
the cistern lever made from my Meccano;
the coal-fired boiler in the kitchen,
its heat, its reek; the fuse box, oh the fuse box,
that time it glowed, not blowing when it should,
my dad, no electrician, turning off
a red-hot mains switch with a broom;
the bomb-cracked wall alive
with electricity, my dad's makeshift
ugly bypass of the broken conduit.
The house where I was born
is in my head. I do not knock.

Steve Francis

Double acrostic sonnet

You ought to go, I know it's time,
our race is run, we're through and I'm
upset it's ending but you too
are done. There's nothing left to loot
remaining in this store. It's hard
each time we say farewell – ta-ta –
auf wiedersehen – so long – goodbye –
let's face the truth, our love has died;
if only you'd agree I'm due
vacation time, a break, a slower
eventual end with hope of a
beginning once again with you
until we work things out, but no
this is our final, final day.

Nigel Kent

Note to Self

We can't repair
a tear in silk
without the stitches
being seen.

Neither can we glue
a mirror split in two
and think it will
reflect the same.

Nor fix the crease
that spoils the corner
of the page
by smoothing it away.

Perhaps we should
embrace the breaks,
the wear and tear
the damage done.

Celebrate the cracks
and chips and nicks
with lacquer
and with gold.

Find a beauty
in brokenness
and not restore,
discard or start anew.

Ivan McGuinness

Misericord

It was an odd thing for us to do. For us, on a Sunday afternoon, to leave the kitchen, the kettle, the loosely rolled spliffs, step beyond the misted windows into the wet leaves and wispy rain. Then go to church. We walked together easily with thumbs hitched to each other's belt loops. Floppy flares dampening and darkening about our ankles, scraping and fraying in the mush of leaves. *We are pilgrims*. You thought about it and said, *Saints and sinners, yeah*. Your hair was bobbled with tiny shiny bubbles of wetness. My fingers forked up the side of your head; it was wet and your hair was suddenly slick. You kissed me. Cold hands, wet white faces, hot wet tongues. On the stone of Wm. Freaker, we sat. *Snick, snick*, said the lighter and we smoked a cheeky single skinner. I pulled a whitey and sat still for nearly days, while you talked of kneelers and pews and my mouth filled like an estuary. *Come inside, this porch is Norman*. I couldn't stop laughing then and asked you if the stone steps were Stanley. Incense, wax and prayer ghosts were surrounded by silence. A dry dead leaf turned slowly on a holy cobweb in the corner of a red and blue window. You tipped a seat up and showed me the fat face of a man, his fat cheeks cupped in his fat fingers, a curious flatness to his head. *Rest your bum on this*. You knelt and tilted your head to me and I was as cold as spring water – then right there in my middle, as hot as the vapour that comes before clouds and water. I laid my hands on your head and said your name, quickly, quietly.

Denis Ahern

Lenny and Lisa

Ooh, his name was Leonardo da Vinci,
Big Lenny to his friends.
He could carve and he could draw
Like no one ever saw
In the art world before or since.
His lady's name was Lisa.
She was a malcontent.
The folks who had known her
Called her the moaner,
Moaner Lisa, Big Lenny's friend.

Polly Stretton

1973 – Bopping at the Rose and Crown

She's behind the bar dancing to the tune of drinkers,
pivoting with pints.
She shimmies a sassy samba, slides to spirits,
jives beside juices,
moves to a sweet minuet for the mixers.

Her arms stretch
with the lime polo neck skinny rib
that rises as she reaches.
The boozers drink her with their eyes,
they wait impatient for their turn,
rounds she memorises without effort,
    Same again? she smiles as they approach.

The tang of alcohol mixes with the stench of cigarette smoke,
yeasty beer, lager, cider, and others that loiter.
Liqueurs in cocktails she mixes without fuss;
no 'Cocktail' moves for her, she'll leave flamboyance to Tom
when 1988 comes along.

The tipplers flirt and she does her job,
smiling, friendly, but not overly so.
She circles, collecting glasses, grinning at jokes
even though she's heard them over and over and...

Tips pile up on the till.

At closing time, she flicks a final pirouette
around the pub,
gathers stray glasses, lifts crisp packets,
nut foils, rubbish from the hubbub of the night;
she swabs the tabletops,
fills the dishwasher, sets it for a last time,
escapes into the arms of Ali waiting outside
and whispers into her ear,
    I hate that fucking job!

Liz Beber

Roles of Fat

In 1978 Susie Orbach published her book Fat is a Feminist Issue

Fat is an adipose tissue.
A metabolic symphony of excess
lining the pockets of our every recess
with packets of energy
put aside as insurance
against a hypothetical hungry day.

Fat is a demographist's issue.
Brown, beige and white
vie in the melting pot of metabolism.
The Falstaffian frame once the privilege
of the prosperous now the stigmata of the skint.
Cursed are the poor in financial planning
for they shall eat carbs.

Fat was a fashionista's virtue.
But tastes change.
Rubenesque curvaceous visions
of sensuous cellulite pale
to stark, wasted Lowrys.
Buck the trend and risk being stuck
At the won't-get-a-date weight.

Fat is a capitalist's profit:
tape worms and thyroxine;
fen-phen amphetamines;
gastric bands and bypass;
WW's calorie counted accounting;
Spanx and beauty bloggers abound.
Big knickers fuel Big Pharma.
Say hello slim, fat – Weygovy™ bye.

How many feminists does it take to change
society's perception of a fat girl?
Back in 1978 around ten percent of kids
were obese. Nowadays it's at least one quarter.
I was always ahead of my time
but there was still no chance
any lad would've asked me to the school dance.

Sue Spiers

Addressing Sylvia Plath's Fan Club

You will need four hundred items in the stew of her:
cumin, lemon, colocynth, bitter apple, lime, broccoli
to get the aftertaste she would want in your memory.

Mix half the ingredients, the dry, dyed ingredients,
cochineal, dates, grasshoppers, bleached flour,
into a cream clay bowl. Wind and wind a spoon

until you cannot tell one ingredient from another
except the black pinpricks of poppy seeds glaring
darkly from the depths of the cream clay bowl.

Take her wet ingredients – rain, brine, absinthe,
sour milk, red wine, all the juices of a basted pig.
Find a few strange ingredients no one else uses.

Let them smoke like *Rauchkäse*, jerky or kippers
while their flavour gets stronger, play her games
with the construction of heavy batter as a side-dish.

Use your mouth and tongue, your teeth and throat.
Chew and swallow. Don't choke on consonants.
Eat her piece by acid piece. Do not spit her out.

Alice Harrison

Best Friends

Two little girls living in an unmade street
played amongst grass, daisies, buttercups, dandelions,
four-leafed clover and calcified dog turds.
The sun shone all summer
and it snowed every winter.

As they grew they made dens.
bounced balls and skipped ropes to rhymes,
stoically suffered skinned knees,
played house, school, doctors and nurses,
linked arms to the corner shop.

They collected marbles, conkers, cigarette cards,
had each other round to tea
with tomato, and egg and cress sandwiches,
made each other laugh so much
food came down their noses.

Older, they built bonfires, lit fireworks, made guys,
carol-sang the neighbourhood,
joined Girl Guides, youth club, theatre club,
went dancing, roller-skating, swimming
and were always sent to Sunday School.

Older still, they cycled for miles,
played cricket and football on waste ground,
swam and dodged waves in the sea,
were stung by nettles, wasps and, once, jellyfish,
hung out in gangs, played kiss-catch.

Then came the eleven-plus.
One passed, one didn't.
New friendships were formed in new schools
until they did little more
than shout *hiya* across the street.

Sally James

Mothers and Daughters

That was when you really belonged to her
then, when she had just ironed your dresses
and your little knickers were airing on
the clothes maiden in the sunshine and
you were crying because you thought
she didn't love you as much as your brother.

It was then that she loved you the most
but you didn't realise it at the time.
Now, when you holiday abroad and your
children's children call you grandma
and she doesn't hear from you for days
she still loves you, though you still think
she prefers your brother to you.

Don't you realise that it is now
that she needs you the most, just like you
needed her all those years ago.
Now when her bones ache and steps
falter and her tears are only a blink away.
Mothers and daughters belong to each other
can't you see it? It is there in the genes.
It can never be altered.

Wendy Goulstone

Solo

The promotions woman
looked me in the eyes
with a steadiness that said:
You can do it,
as beside me he went on at length
how he hated jazz
always had, always would
wild horses wouldn't drag him there,
et cetera.
I wasn't enamoured either
but there was a principal at stake here
when that look passed between us
I had already made up my mind.

She was taking tickets at the gate.
I knew you would come, she said,
*I would have been disappointed
if you hadn't come.*
She wasn't talking about missing a sale.

An ancient Greek style amphitheatre,
fairy lights in the trees. Idyllic.
Pianist, saxophonist, bass player,
the world-famous vibraphonist
I had never heard of.
I learned a great deal that night
about jazz, about improvisation,
about playing solo.

Adrian Green

At the Philharmonic

That silence
    that is not silence
    before the music starts
filling the hall
    with sound
that is not sound
but a buzz
    of whispered conversation
    throat-clearing coughs
and the oboe's A
clear above the scrapes and toots
    of orchestral adjustment
and when the oboe stops
    that quiet of no sound
    except the embarrassment
    of left-over sentences
before the symphony begins.

Katherine Rawlings

STARLINGS

Blue dusk a murmuration of starlings
As they mass they swirl, turn and swoop
They wheel and waltz without colliding
Each moves to the centre of the group
Thus they billow up to several thousand
A wonder of nature riding high
Crossing continents, seas and mountains
Confusing predators in the sky
The bigger birds can't single them out
A beautiful scheme in nature's plan
Yet when they rest they become a blight
As they mess and chitter annoying man
Aloft in the sunset they enthrall
On the ground their abstract art appalls

M. C. Gardner

what gifts?

I dream and drift
by the waterfall

under the fir trees are
grasses for the goats

in the meadows spin
too many angry insects

clouds turn scarlet as
shadows hang above the river

my dream nurses a storm
of my own as I trip and fall

Dan Sarkozi

A whisper of heavy wings

A Haiku Inspired by Karen Macfarlane's Haibun:

a sole swan
sailing through mist —
there's no nest this year

Julie Anne Gilligan

CORMORANT

An object of tension, a movement in white: gulls
agitate, a snow flake flurry of erratic flight.

Dark as sea wrack, a stock-still silhouette
stands guard on the shallows, watches
over the shoals. He cultivates indifference
with a nonchalant stance: too much
for the rabble, the bragging of gulls.

They're beating their wings, indignant,
fretting, 'til the sentinel decides
enough is enough: granite-grey wings
spread wide to their limit, to other
dimensions, other meals, other tides.

He calls an orderly halt to their petty pride:
motion becomes murmur, squabbles subside.

Sally Evans

A djinn-eyed clan

tastes the addled breath of a sleeping city
as they mark its flesh-filled baskets,
monochrome under a hunter's moon.

The chittering pack sees patchwork
alleys bleed; hear sweet-iron whistles scent
the air as the city streets grow still.

Her pink slash smile spikes a long-box neck.
Spice dries her throat and dusts the road.
Coffee creases her nose.

With one quick flick of a black-brush tail
their saffron-spotted queen summons them.
Hyena enter Harar-Gey.

Susan Jarvis Bryant

Ode to an Opossum

You skulk as starlight oozes through the leaves
To dapple fur in ripples of the night.
Marble-statue-still I see you freeze –
Your alabaster face, a ghostly sight.
Your glinting eyes of jet as sharp as flint –
Two beady ebon gems where moonbeams revel.
I marvel at your snoopy, rosy nose
All slick and flecked with muck – a sticky hint
Of juicy nasties grubbing muzzles shovel
From depths where pulpous morsels decompose.

I've seen you playing dead to stay alive.
I ponder on the corpses of your kin
All rigor-mortis stiff. Did each survive
The Reaper's scythe? Your thespian within
(That legend of the death-defying day)
Intrigues me with that drop-and-drool routine:
The curl of claw, the reek of rot – a smell
From hell that keeps rapacious beasts at bay –
A scene to faze the meanest drama queen.
It serves your scheming genus very well.

But, most of all I laud and I applaud
Just what your wacky habits do for me.
I see beyond the eerie-featured fraud
To bright and bug-free, backyard harmony.
Your jaws will gnaw on vile and viscid critters –
Those that squirm and scuttle through the grass.
Your fruitful, rooting snout will never miss
A crunchy lunch that gives me fits of jitters.
Marsupial of the cockroach-munching class,
You bless my life with warm, alfresco bliss.

Poets

Name	Page	Name	Page
Pip Adwin	9	Sally James	45
Denis Ahern	37	Susan Jarvis Bryant	53
K. J. Barrett	27	Nigel Kent	35
Liz Beber	40	Jim Lindop	32
Ian Campbell	16	Jacob Lund	14
Geoff Chilton	15	Karen Macfarlane	10
Cate Cody	22	Ross McGivern	7
Phil Craddock	18	Ivan McGuinness	36
Barbara Cumbers	33	Suzie Millar	31
Sally Evans	52	Kewal Paigankar	13
Tim Field	26	Katherine Rawlings	48
Steve Francis	34	Dee Richards	24
M. C. Gardner	49	Dan Sarkozi	50
Julie Anne Gilligan	51	Ian Simmonds	17
Wendy Goulstone	46	Sue Spiers	42
Adrian Green	47	Polly Stretton	38
Jenny Hamlett	20	Tony Sutton	29
Alice Harrison	43	Kate Young	28
Helen Hunniset	23		

Acknowledgements:

'The Grey' by Pip Adwin was first published in *Dreich Magazine* #100A

'Note to Self' by Nigel Kent first appeared in *Dreich Magazine* #100A and subsequently in his collection: *Sent* (Hedgehog Press)

'A Prophecy' by Jacob Lund was first published in *Acoustic Mirrors*, Spectral Pixels Press, 2024.

'When You Need Courage for the Year Ahead' by Karen Macfarlane was first published on the OU Poetry website and then in Karen's collection *All about the Surface* (Seahorse Publications)

'Addressing Sylvia Plath's Fan Club' by Sue Spiers appears on the Ink, Sweat and Tears website: https://inksweatandtears.co.uk/sue-spiers-and-mike-huett-for-day-three-of-our-archive-feature/

www.ingramcontent.com/pod-product-compliance
Lightning Source LLC
Chambersburg PA
CBHW061344040426
42444CB00011B/3083